SUPERWOMAN

The 7 Ways to a

Successful Career Woman and Loving Mom

Annette C. Breuer

ISBN-13:
978-1721016914

ISBN-10:
1721016910

I would like to dedicate this book to all working mothers who love being moms, partners and friends, but who are also on fire for their careers, who try their best to balance career and family, who tackle their challenge with heart and soul and dive 100% into the adventure of a working mom, trying all the while, to keep their heads above water.

CONTENTS

Before our first child was born, I was convinced that I was going to go straight back to work, and not take any time off. Therefore, I had already organized a place at a creche nearby. Okay – everything was planned! The baby could come! I was ready. But, pretty soon, I realized, first of all, that with children, things never go as planned, especially when they are small, and secondly, we also change, whether we admit it right away or need time to come to the point of realization. And I do not mean to be judgmental – I'm merely stating a fact.

In my case, I quickly found out that a creche simply wasn't an option, because I felt that it would be better to let my child grow up at home – so, I organized a babysitter and arranged my life accordingly. I set up an office and coordinated the various processes to suit my family life. Over the years – the second child was already there – I didn't actually realize how demanding it is to balance life and career, especially if one tends towards perfectionism and has a strong sense of responsibility, and is very conscientious on top of that. I reached my personal limits more and more often, but I still loved both my job and being a mother. I felt more and more empty all the time, began to simply function and no longer had the joie de vivre I should have had.

What was the reason?
Was I unable to cope with my life?
Did I need to work even harder?
Were the others to blame, my family,
my partner, the system?
Did I have the wrong expectations?

Question upon question – I was running around in circles and getting nowhere, until I was given a tip – I needed personal support, from a coach. "Okay, I guess I could give it a try!" But that was the turning point in my life. Since then, there has been so much positive change in my life, for myself, for my family and for my career, and it just keeps moving forward.

To help other wonderful women, who want to balance family and career without letting anything fall by the wayside, who want to find their own personal route to success, I have put together seven significant steps that every loving, successful career mom should take to heart.

1. YOUR PERSONAL VALUES AND DEEPEST CONVICTIONS

When I speak about values, it's not only about moral values – first and foremost, I am referring to your own concept of values and behavior, the things you value highly and which give you a sense of purpose and satisfaction in life. If you are aware of your personal values and live according to them, you will enjoy an overall sense of well-being. You won't feel the need to compare yourself with others and you will not be open to attack. You will be able to listen to critical remarks and provocations, and then decide whether or not the criticism is justified, and whether or not you are prepared to take it to heart or reject it as information that does not need to be processed any further. Our values help us to achieve a higher level of willpower and courage and protect us from negative and destructive influences. In order to identify your personal values and your deepest convictions, it is useful to consider the following questions:

1. Which behaviors and habits annoy you intensely in other people?

It's highly probably, that the exact opposite is one of your most important values.

An example: You are at a meeting and one of your colleagues ignores you, he interrupts you, he doesn't let you finish speaking, he doesn't listen to what you are saying, he takes over the conversation – that could annoy you, because that kind of behavior is disrespectful, ignorant, arrogant and impolite. Therefore, you can conclude that politeness or respect are generally very important personal values in your life.

It isn't about generally applicable definitions, but rather about the way you see it personally. Accordingly, for you, values such as family, trust and honesty, or friendship, loyalty and integrity, could be important. Take the time to reflect on disturbing situations, so that you can investigate why you felt angry or hurt.

2. Where does your passion lie, what do you find exciting, what do you stand for (uncompromis-ingly), what are you prepared to fight for and what values do you associate with the above?

3. What do you want to teach your children about what matters in life – which values and convictions do you consider essential?

LIVE YOUR VALUES

Every day, we experience situations in which we have the opportunity to make decisions regarding which route we want to take. I call them decision points. Every decision point gives you the opportunity to put your "why" into practice, and to live the way you want to. The more you decide to act according to your deepest convictions and values, the more vital, effective, fulfilled and meaningful your life will become, and the quicker you will reach your goals.

CONFLICTING GOALS

Very often, we find ourselves in situations in which we are torn between two possibilities that are equally important to us – our job versus our children – considering yourself or your family. The key is to see the choice between the options not as *better* or *worse*, but rather as *equally important* and *different*. Then, you make a decision, not because one option is better than the other, but rather because you have to make a decision. Sometimes, making a decision can be very difficult and challenging. For example, if you have to go on a business trip, but it's going to mean missing your son's birthday party. Then, you assess the value of "doing a good job, being able to pay the bills and giving your family a pleasant life". You can look for other possible ways to express your other value, namely, "being a loving parent". You could organize a party before or after your trip, Skype with your son on his birthday or send him a video message.

Living your values doesn't mean that your life is going to be free of challenges and difficulties.

It isn't easy, and it's usually not much fun, at least not at the moment in which you have to decide. But living in such a way that you can prize your own values and convictions and integrate them into your life, is the price you pay for a meaningful life that makes sense and is full of happy moments.

If you know who you are and what you stand for, then you deal with the most important decisions in your life with the most powerful tool of all:

Your "self", your personality.

2. YOUR LIFE PURPOSE – WHY IS IT WORTH GETTING UP EVERY DAY TO CARRY ON?

For most people, it is not easy to capture the sense of life – of our lives – in words. But one day, when you finally know what it is, you'll find it's worth getting up every day, having a goal to work towards, never giving up, even if the hill you want to climb is steep and full of obstacles. And knowing why you do what you do, will enable you to summon the courage to carry on. It gives you staying power and courage, because you know why you're doing it in the first place. Then the lightness will return to your life, and you will be able to motivate yourself again, even after setbacks and difficulties. Your life purpose is like a thread from which you can draw orientation. Ideally, it should be closely aligned to your values, and it should describe what you want to achieve in life.

HOW DO I FIND THE ANSWER?

Finding your purpose in life, and answering the question as to why you are on this earth, is a process. The more you think about it consciously and recognize who you are, what's really important to you, where your passion lies, what your character traits, strengths and talents are, what's important to you in life, what gives you a feeling of fulfillment, what you are able to achieve and what you want to achieve personally, the clearer and more precise the answers will become with time.

There are many possibilities to come closer to your purpose in life and to capture your motto for life in the form of a statement. You can meditate, keep a diary, read or indulge in conversation with people who are important to you. Here are some more suggestions:

Imagine that you could turn back time to a point in your life when you were totally contented, when you felt that nothing could go wrong, when you were full of drive, motivated, positive, happy, excited. You didn't care what others thought of you, you felt absolutely alive and invincible. Where were you? What were you doing? Who was with you? What impact did you have on your environment? What did you trigger in others? What mattered to you?

Or, project yourself into the future. What would you like to have written in your eulogy? What legacy do you want to leave behind as a person, how do you want to be remembered, what do you want to achieve before you die, what has your contribution been to making this world a better place and what would you like your children, your family, friends and acquaintances to say about you?

You can also try this: boast a little. How courageous were you? How clever were you and how wisely did you act? How well did you chair the meeting or how well do you raise and guide your child?

Boast about what a great mom you are, because you did all of those things well! Those were moments in which you had an impact, moments that say a whole lot about your attitude towards life.

Look for opportunities to search yourself deeply, listen to yourself and be honest with yourself.

If you don't like (guided) inner journeys, then ask yourself critical questions, work with tables that depict your talents, your most fulfilled moments, your needs or your assessment models. Be like a 3-year old who constantly asks: "Why?", "Why?" and never stop digging deeper and deeper. Then, try to formulate your life purpose, your personal goal.

One of my trainers formulated her life purpose like this:

I'm the sharp pebble in a shoe, that pricks me and others again and again, in order to bring out the best in myself and others and to utilize my/their potential to the fullest.

And one of my clients found her purpose in bringing "more love" into the world, in encouraging herself and others, in being authentic and never giving up.

Another motto for life is: "I am the light in the world that makes people laugh and brings more joy into the world."

However you formulate your life purpose, it certainly doesn't need to be an epic quote or a perfectly formulated statement. Your life purpose must be clear and unambiguous to yourself, not to other people. It's all about you!

Your life purpose reflects your deepest conviction(s) and passions, lends you stability and acts like a compass that guides you back onto the right path, again and again.

3. THE PATH TO YOUR GOAL

The first time I was challenged to think about how I implement my life purpose, I thought to myself: "Oh! That's easy!", and then, I realized that it wasn't all that clear and simple, after all. I had a total mental block. I started rethinking what my life purpose meant to me personally, in my everyday life. I tried to find examples from my professional and private life, and instead of positive examples, most of the situations and experiences I came up with were examples of how it shouldn't be, or of how I wasn't living my life purpose. Expressing your life purpose and acting accordingly in one's everyday life is challenging. We allow external circumstances to influence us and fall back into old behavior patterns and habits, we let our fears get the upper hand, and we become weary, exhausted, and shy away from making major decisions and structural changes. This is absolutely normal – it's part of the process. But, the decisive factor is to just keep going and to say to ourselves: "So far and no further. From now on, I'm going to try again, and do my best!" You'll discover that it works! It might take a while, because it's going to mean doing some work on yourself, getting rid of old habits and developing new awareness. Sometimes, this is very demanding, but step by step, you'll come closer to your goal. And, if you need support, ask for help. It's nothing to be ashamed of! Quite to the contrary: asking for help shows intelligence and strength, because, even though, as a Superwoman, we often believe that we can do everything on our own, that is a misconception and it is not one of the characteristics of a successful career mom. Asking for help and accepting it means stepping out of your comfort zone, especially for independent people who are used to taking things into their own hands. But it's worth it, and it represents a significant piece of the puzzle on the way to reaching one's life goal. On the way, you are going to encounter setbacks again and again. Try to see them as a gift, because they will give you the chance to pause inwardly, think about what has happened, learn from it and discover what doesn't work, what isn't good for you or where you need to change something. When you have discovered and formulated your life purpose, this will become your anchor, especially if you get to the point, once again, where you find yourself asking: "Why am I doing all of this?"

POSSIBLE IMPLEMENTATION METHODS

Write down your life purpose on a large sheet of paper or cardboard, give it a creative design, according to your taste, and put it up somewhere where you can see it and read it several times a day. Then, start looking for opportunities to express your life purpose. Make a list of at least 25 alternatives, as to how you would like to implement your life purpose. Perhaps changes to the structure of your professional or private life. Or possibly projects or dreams that you want to achieve. Maybe just taking 5 – 10 peaceful minutes a day for yourself, for example, enjoying a cup of coffee before the usual chaos begins. Don't wait too long before starting to compile your list and set yourself a strict time limit within which it must be completed. Select the two activities from the list, which interest you the most, and put down at least three steps you need to take in order to implement them. It also makes sense to set deadlines by which these steps should be completed. Then get started! Don't wait any longer! Life is much too precious and beautiful to simply stand there watching it pass by.

4. ENOUGH OF OLD STORIES AND LIMITING BELIEFS

I am convinced that all people come to points in their lives, where they realize that they are standing in their own way – perhaps because they have been influenced by their upbringing in one way or another; perhaps because, due to past experiences, they have – consciously or unconsciously – adopted character traits or convictions that are no longer any use to them; perhaps because they are still burdened by old stories that are causing a blockage.

Regardless of the reason why we feel that we are standing in our own way, we need to face these issues and deal with them. Only when we manage to sort out those old stories and get rid of those limiting convictions (beliefs) will we be free for something new, and able to live a carefree, self-confident life. If we don't do so, these things will catch up with us, again and again, especially if we are under a lot of pressure, or feeling tired or sensitive. Of course, these beliefs and the emotions they generate, behave like little leprechauns, who flick the switch at exactly the right moment, when we are feeling weak, then giggle into their sleeves as they watch us doing the same old things, over and over again:

You rush home after a hard day at work and a heated argument with a colleague, knowing that you still have to do the washing and bake a birthday cake for your son. You unlock the door and your daughter rushes towards you cheerfully, because she still needs the right blouse for her riding tournament the next day. You open the fridge and discover, with shock, that you don't have enough eggs for the cake, although you were absolutely certain that there were plenty. You start planning the next steps frantically, and the phone rings – your mother. When you try to explain to her that you don't have time to talk, she replies snappily: "You never have any time! Are you in a state of stress again? It's all too much for you …" ta-daaa – and the story begins all over again. You feel as though you're under attack, under pressure, and you become furious, feel unappreciated, would love to hang up on her, perhaps you even start arguing with your mom and you snap at your children. Then, those old beliefs come up again: "I'm not good enough", "I'm not going to succeed anyway", "I'm never going to manage", "Without me, nothing functions". We start digging up old family stories, some of which we didn't even have anything to do with, but which has encroached into our family lives and become firmly integrated within us or our lives, making it impossible to distance ourselves from it.

Beliefs develop, either consciously or unconsciously, from experiences, which we assess and associate with emotions. They form our very specific view of a matter, and this influences the way we deal with it. Limiting beliefs usually prevent us from wanting to gather new experiences, thereby robbing us of the opportunity to revise them. If we are not aware of them, we feel that we are in a vicious circle that has no end, in which the same thing happens over and over again. The only way to get out of this situation is to take an intensive look at the way you see things, and to develop a new point of view.

I orient myself according to Byron Katie's questions. Choose one of the beliefs that is hampering you, e.g. "I am an overburdened superior", or "I am a bad mother", and write down the answers to the following five questions:

1. Is this really true?
(Yes or no? If you answered no, go to question 3).

2. Can you absolutely know that it's true?
(Yes or no?)
The answers to questions 1 and 2 are monosyllabic, simple and free of additional explanations. It is important that you are honest with yourself when answering these questions.

3. How do you react? What will happen, if you believe these statements? What emotions do you feel? How does your body react, where do you feel the emotion(s)? How do you react and deal with yourself and others?

Let a typical situation relating to this limiting belief run through your mind, and immerse yourself in this moment, as best you can. Perceive all of the reactions, that rise up within you when you believe the statements: "I am an overburdened superior" or "I am a bad mother". With these questions, you can begin to perceive the inner causes and effects. You are able to recognize that, when you believe these statements, it results in an uncomfortable feeling, a burden that can range from mild discomfort to fear and panic.

4. What is good about this belief?

What do you gain from it?

This may be a confusing question, but it is intended to give you more clarity and to get to the core of the belief. Be curious.

5. Who would you be without that thought?

What would it be like if this belief had never existed? What would be different for you?

How would you feel if you didn't have this idea in your head?

Now, consider who you would be in the same situation, without that idea: "I am an overburdened superior" or "I am a bad mother". Who would you be or what would you be like in the same situation, if you did not believe this statement? Close your eyes and imagine the typical situation we spoke about earlier. Take your time. Take careful note of what comes to mind. How do you see it now? What do you feel? How would you behave? Do you notice the difference?

In this way, your consciousness is able to develop the necessary insight for a new belief.

Now, try to find a new, appropriate way to formulate it. It should make you feel harmonious and pleasant and it shouldn't be longer than one sentence.

5. STRUCTURE – EVERYDAY TIPS AND TRICKS

Unfortunately, the day only has 24 hours, and annoying as it may be, we also have to sleep a bit, so that we are able to fulfill the great expectations we have of ourselves, at least to some extent – being a successful career woman and a cheerful, loving and understanding mom, not to mention our other roles as a partner, daughter and friend. If you don't want to fall by the wayside entirely, you need to structure your day, set priorities and do something to make your everyday life simpler.

Begin by observing yourself – how many hours of sleep do you need to feel fit? You can cope with too little sleep for quite a long time, but you will notice yourself becoming more and more irritable and sensitive, and you'll find your joie de vivre and lightness diminishing every day and the challenges you face growing into indomitable monsters. Next, determine when you are most productive. Are you more of an early riser or a night-owl? Do you like to sit down at your desk in the evenings, after the family has settled down for the night, or do you prefer to get up early and use the time before everyone else gets up?

I always used to think that the best time for me to work was in the evenings and late at night.

But meanwhile, I have discovered, and admitted to myself, that I'm actually an early riser. I enjoy watching the sunrise and listening to the birds singing while everything else around me is very quiet. Before the rest of the world wakes up, I have already achieved a lot, and I still have the whole day ahead of me. Once you've sorted out these two issues for yourself, you will know, firstly, when your day should begin, and secondly, how many hours are available for all the other things the day has in store for you.

Now, you need to plan your week. First of all, draw up a list of all the things that you normally do – the things you have to do on a regular basis. Plan in your leisure time, your sporting activities and time for yourself. Then, design a timetable, with the days of the weeks and the hours, and enter the activities accordingly. You'll probably find that there isn't enough space for all the things you've put on your list. When it comes to the activities over which you have an influence, you need to ask yourself which of them you actually want to do, when you want to or should do them and how often you have to give something up or need to arrange for someone to help or support you. Set priorities and learn to take things calmly. I know that's easier said than done, but I promise you, it can be done, and with a little practice and routine, you'll find that it's a significant step towards achieving happiness, satisfaction and pleasure in life.

An example of a daily schedule:

5.00	Get up
5.30 - 6.30	Compile my daily list of priorities, emails, social media
6.30 - 8.00	Family (breakfast, children, morning routine)
8.00 - 8.30	Emails, structuring my workday
8.30 - 1pm	Work
1.00 - 2pm	Lunch break, emails
2.00 - 4pm	Work
4.00 – 7pm	Private
7.00 – 8pm	Dinner / evening routine

Your daily priority list should contain all of the activities that you want to do on that day, including telephone calls. Add the letters A, B and C to the individual points, and make a separate column in which you can check the tasks that you have completed. You can also prepare your daily activity list the evening before. Try to find out what fits best into the rhythm of your life.

It might look really easy, and in principle it is just that. But the greatest challenge is breaking down your tasks to fit into this daily plan, and then also sticking to your plan. That means, for example, only taking time for emails, Facebook and Instagram at the appointed times. You should also try to avoid doing several things at once. Rather concentrate on one task or project and finish it before you move onto the next point on your list. Also plan in fixed time windows for doctor's appointments (dentist, checkups etc.), visits to the hairdresser or bookkeeping, and be strict about keeping them free for just that! Strive for household support. This could be in form of a cleaner, a robotic vacuum cleaner, help with the ironing or a delivery service for your groceries. Include your family; make your children and your partner responsible for some of the chores and plan the week together, in advance. And, when planning, always keep in mind those things that have the highest priority in your life at that moment, remembering to consider your personal values and your life purpose while you're about it.

6. EMOTIONAL INTELLIGENCE AND FLEXIBILITY

We want our lives to be as awesome as possible, without any emotional pain, but life is made up of light and shadow – the beauty of life is directly connected to your fragility. That means not seeing emotions as good or bad, but simply as they are, or as what they are – an emotion. Emotions don't need to be fixed, controlled or fought! We don't have to do anything more than simply welcome the inner experience, and to breathe them in and explore their contours, without trying to expel them as quickly as we can. You can't choose or control your wishes, desires and longings. But you can decide whether or not you're going to light the next cigarette, you can decide whether or not you're going to have a second bowl of dessert and you can decide whether or not you're going to go home with someone you've just met at a bar. If you are emotionally agile, you don't waste any energy wrestling with impulses. You simply make decisions according to what matters to you. In this regard, it's important that you can put a name to your emotions, as precisely as possible. People who are able to identify the full range of emotions, who are able to recognize the difference between sadness and boredom, self-pity, loneliness or upheaval, for example, are usually much better able to cope with the highs and lows of normal life than those who only see it as black or white.

People who have emotional intelligence and flexibility are able to tolerate high stress levels and cope with setbacks, whilst remaining committed, open and curious. They understand that life has its highs and lows – but they don't give up. They simply keep pursuing their long-term goals, in harmony with their deepest convictions. They also have emotions like fear, anger and disappointment, but they meet them with curiosity, self-empathy and acceptance.

Achieving emotional intelligence and flexibility is a process that makes it possible to be 100 % present and to retain or change our behavior so that we are able to live in a way that harmonizes with our goals, intentions and values. This process is not about ignoring or suppressing difficult emotions and unpleasant thoughts. It's about accepting one's emotions and thoughts, facing up to them courageously, and then getting over them, so that great things can happen in our lives. The process of emotional intelligence and flexibility unfolds in four important steps:

1. SHOWING UP

This means being willing to face up to your thoughts, emotions and habits with curiosity and understanding.

Good questions that you can ask yourself if you want to learn from your emotions are:

"What are the intentions behind this emotion?"

"What is it telling me?", "What do I gain from it?",

"What is causing this sadness, frustration, joy?"

2. STEPPING OUT

The next element is to separate yourself from the thoughts and emotions and to see them for what they are – simply thoughts, simply emotions.

One of many exercises:

Many studies have shown that writing is a proven method in the process of dealing with your emotions. People who write about an emotionally loaded incident experience a noticeable improvement to both their emotional and physical wellbeing. They are happier and less depressed, and they worry less. Writing not only helps you to work through things. It also helps you to find your way out of your despondent, defeated, paralyzed state and become active once again. Stepping out and putting your emotions into words is an extremely helpful way to deal with stress, worry and loss. The process of writing gives one the opportunity to put some distance between the thinker and the thoughts, the feeler and the feelings, so that we are able to develop a new perspective, to free ourselves and to make progress.

Pennebaker's Writing Rules (Professor at the University of Texas):

Set a timer for 20 minutes. Take a writing pad or work on your computer. When the timer begins, start writing about your emotional experiences over the past week, month and year. Don't worry about punctuation, writing style, etc. Simply write, and let your thoughts lead you wherever they want to. Remain curious and don't assess what you have written. Simply write for yourself and not for any possible reader. Do this for several days, then throw the piece of paper away, delete the document or start a blog. It doesn't really matter. The decisive factor is that these thoughts have now come out of you, out of your head, and are on that piece of paper. So, you have started the process of stepping out of your experiences, in order to gain another perspective of them.

3. WALKING YOUR WHY

Finally, focus on what's really important to you – your deepest personal values and goals – then answer the following question:

"What do I really want, and why?"

4. MOVING ON

a.) <u>The tiny tweak principle</u>:

And finally, it's not about making radical changes to your life, but rather making little, deliberate tweaks, based on your values. They can make an enormous difference in your life. This is particularly the case when they manage to break through your routine and your habits – this can initiate an incredible leverage on the changes in your life.

For example, combine a new habit with an old one: eat fruit with your muesli. Leave your mobile phone in your study when you want to spend some quality time with your children. Turn your afternoon coffee break into a team event, and make use of the opportunity for some personal exchange with your colleagues.

b.) The see-saw principle:

The see-saw principle means constantly finding the balance between challenges and skills, so that we are neither complacent nor overwhelmed, but rather passionate, enthusiastic and strengthened by the challenges we face.

Emotional intelligence is not going to make you into a perfect person who never says the wrong thing and is never overwhelmed by emotions of fear, shame or anger.

But emotional intelligence and flexibility lead to less misunderstandings and stress, and more fun and success in your private and professional life, and they make a huge contribution towards achieving a better quality of life.

7. REFLECTION – MEDITATION – TIMEOUT

Our everyday lives as successful career woman, mom and partner are often packed so full that we flop onto the sofa in the evening, stretch our legs out in front of us and start skipping through the television channels aimlessly, unwilling to formulate any thoughts at all in our minds. But, even if we finally had a little time to ourselves, and could just ignore those mountains of laundry, the papers on our desks or the toys in the living room, we wouldn't have the energy or the will to use the time for ourselves, personally, to do something that does us good, to switch off or to do something that energizes us. That's why it's so important to pause from time to time, and observe yourself consciously, to perceive the moment and to ask yourself: "What's happening right now? Do I want it? Is it in my best interests? How do I feel? Why? Is it expedient? What is really important to me?"

The way that you consciously take time to reflect,
recuperate or prepare for the day ahead can take
many different forms, depending on the type of
person you are, your daily routine, the life phase
you're in and your possibilities. What's important is
that you consciously take this time to find out what
really does you good, what's helpful for you. One
option is meditation. For me, meditation was something very strange for a long time. It felt like a coat
that was too big for me, that I could lose myself in,
that didn't fit me. But it still fascinated me when I
read about the positive effects of meditation or
heard about them from so many people who
meditate regularly. I also thought that meditating
took a very long time. Where was I going to find
time to fit it in? Meanwhile, I have come to understand that meditation can take on a wide range of
forms, and that it doesn't only mean sitting in the
lotus position on a yoga mat. You can also do it very
effectively and easily for seven minutes every
morning. Meditation, like many other things,

is also a process that we have to allow, but which we can organize ourselves. Try it again and again. Clinical studies show that meditation has a positive effect on our brain. With regular meditation, we are better able to regulate our feelings, which in turn leads to a reduction of the damaging effects of stress hormones on our immune systems.

According to the latest studies, in this way, meditation can also have a positive effect on inflammatory diseases, immunity and even the aging of cells. Furthermore, meditation demonstrably alters parts of the brain and it could even slow down the aging of the brain.

There are many good, guided meditations with a selection of accompanying music. You can use an app or do it your own way. You can meditate in the morning, the afternoon or the evening, every day or a few times a week, at home, in the office, on the train – whatever feels right for you.

Other possibilities for regeneration and reflection could be a one free evening a week, just for you and your needs – that hot cup of tea or coffee to enjoy at leisure or a relaxing candlelight bath with pleasant music. It's important to find out how much time you need to take for yourself, and how often. Then choose those things that will bring you closer to your goal, and implement them consciously.

As time goes by, you'll find that you are becoming more balanced all the time, that you are able to keep an overview of things, that nothing throws you off balance so easily anymore, and that you are able to recognize, in a moment, what's expedient and what really matters right now.

Finally, I would like to add that you cannot successfully change, or adopt new habits overnight – it takes practice. Generally, for something to become a firm habit, you need to do it 21 times – there are varying opinions here, some of which speak of even more repetitions. And if you fall back into your old habits, be gentle with yourself.

It happens to the best of us, and it's absolutely human. After all, we aren't machines that can be quickly reprogrammed – we are humans with a heart and a soul, who simply try to do our best every day. Just start over again, because if you persevere, you will achieve everything you have set out to do.

8. SELF-LOVE – A POEM IN CLOSING

A poem by Charlie Chaplin, which was recited on the occasion of his 70th birthday:

SELF-LOVE

As I began to love myself
I found that anguish and emotional suffering
are only warning signs that I was living
against my own truth.
Today, I know, this is
"AUTHENTICITY".

As I began to love myself
I understood how much it can offend somebody
if I try to force my desires on this person,
even though I knew the time was not right
and the person was not ready for it,
and even though this person was me.
Today I call it
"RESPECT".

As I began to love myself

I stopped craving for a different life,

and I could see that everything

that surrounded me was inviting me to grow.

Today I call it

"MATURITY".

As I began to love myself

I understood that at any circumstance,

I am in the right place at the right time,

and everything happens

at the exactly right moment. So I could be calm.

Today I call it

"SELF-CONFIDENCE".

As I began to love myself

I quit stealing my own time,

and I stopped designing huge project

for the future. Today, I only do what

brings me joy and happiness,

things I love to do and that make my heart cheer,

and I do them in my own way

and in my own rhythm.

Today I call it

"SIMPLICITY".

As I began to love myself

I freed myself of anything

that is no good for my health

– food, people, things, situations,

and everything that drew me down

and away from myself.

At first I called this attitude a healthy egoism.

Today I know it is

"LOVE OF ONESELF".

As I began to love myself

I quit trying to always be right,

and ever since I was wrong less of the time.

Today I discovered that is

"MODESTY".

As I began to love myself

I refused to go on living in the past

and worrying about the future.

Now, I only live for the moment,

where everything is happening.

Today I live each day, day by day, and I call it

"FULFILLMENT".

As I began to love myself

I recognized that my mind can disturb me

and it can make me sick.

But as I connected it to my heart,

my mind became a valuable ally.

Today I call this connection

"WISDOM OF THE HEART".

We no longer need to fear arguments,

confrontations or any kind of problems with

ourselves or others. Even stars collide,

and out of their crashing

new worlds are born.

Today I know

"THAT IS LIFE!"

ABOUT THE AUTHOR

Annette C. Breuer is the founder of
Alaria Coaching.

She was trained and received her certification as a
CPCC at the Coaches Training Institute (CTI).
Before her current career, she was a partner at
HumanCapital – Executive Search.
Annette also worked as a consultant for three years,
and she was employed by an international aviation
company for over ten years.

Qualifications:
Degree in Economic Science
Certified Professional Co-Active Coach
Certified Professional Children's and
Youth Coach (IPE)
Co-Active Leadership
Positive Psychology